IMAGES
of America

SEYMOUR

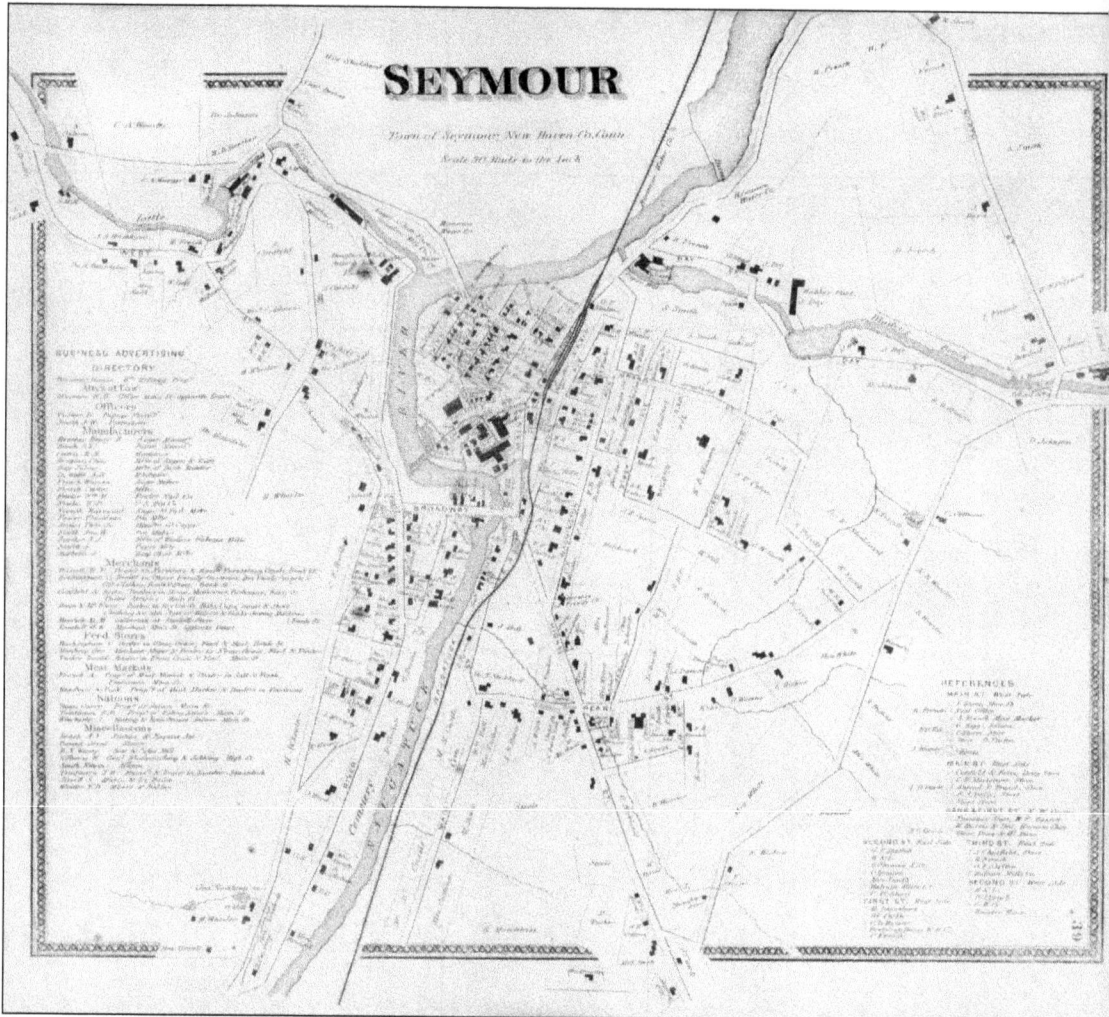

SEYMOUR

This map of Seymour in 1868 shows what the town was like during the early years. Included on the map are a business advertising directory on the left side and a reference legend on the bottom right. Not only does the map show how rural the town was outside of the downtown area, but it shows the area where Second and Third Streets were located by the river. Other streets have changed names; for example, what was known then as High Street is now Maple Street. The map was taken from a county map published by H. and C. T. Smith of Philadelphia in 1856. (Scott Tuttle.)

ON THE COVER: The workers of the Seymour Manufacturing Company walk along the railroad tracks over the Naugatuck River towards downtown Seymour. In this 1902 photograph, the tracks are level with the landscape before Route 67 was established with a train trestle. (Barton Collection.)

IMAGES
of America

SEYMOUR

Theresa W. Conroy

ARCADIA
PUBLISHING

Published by Arcadia Publishing
Charleston, South Carolina

Library of Congress Control Number: 2010921766

For all general information contact Arcadia Publishing at:
Telephone 843-853-2070
Fax 843-853-0044
E-mail sales@arcadiapublishing.com
For customer service and orders:
Toll-Free 1-888-313-2665

Visit us on the Internet at www.arcadiapublishing.com

*To my parents, Francis and Anna Conroy, for teaching me
the value of giving to my community and for sharing her rich
history with me. There truly is no place like home!*

CONTENTS

ACKNOWLEDGMENTS

This book is a combined effort of many people. It could never have been produced without help from my parents, Francis and Anna Conroy. Where there was no written history to be found, they were invaluable in locating and providing the history through their own experiences. Their extensive collection of photographs is used throughout the book and is the source of all unattributed pictures. The diligent work that Marian K. O'Keefe provided in completing a historic resources inventory for the Connecticut Historical Commission in the 1970s became almost an exclusive chapter on historical homes in the town. The Citizens Engine Company No. 2 is a museum unto itself. Walls of historic photographs line the building. A special thank you to all the members who helped get the photographs down and to Capt. Michael Lombardi for arranging it to be done. When a call for photographs went out to residents, many answered: George and Ruth Jarvis, Fred Watton, Scott Tuttle, Robert Lang, Walter Marsh, Steven Pupchyk, Richard Joy, John Felenchak, Randy Stone, Alex Danka, Richard Kisson, Geri Swinik, and others whose photographs and stories were shared with me. After many years, I was able to converse with my third-grade teacher, Winifred Barton, who handed down the collection of her father, Clarence Barton, to be used as a resource. Special thanks to my editor, Hilary Zusman, for keeping me on track with my first project. To my sons, Joe and Frank Niezelski, thank you for all your help and support throughout this process. And finally to William C. Sharpe, who had the foresight and diligence to record Seymour's early history in his 1902 book *Seymour Past and Present*. Without this resource, the history of Seymour truly would have been lost.

INTRODUCTION

The Naugatuck Valley region of Connecticut comprises seven towns/cities, including Ansonia, Beacon Falls, Derby, Naugatuck, Oxford, Seymour, and Shelton. Together, these towns serve as a working region for resources and common heritage and have been awarded the All-American City Award.

Seymour is unique in both its natural and man-made resources. The landscape includes rolling hills, the Naugatuck and Housatonic Rivers, the Waterbury branch line of Metro-North Railroad, and a major thoroughfare, Route 8.

Seymour's recorded history began in 1633, the earliest date used relating to the Indians at the falls on the Naugatuck River. The river has been a focal point throughout the history of Seymour: from the settlement of Indians, to waterpower for manufacturing during the last century, to the current focus of change, to recreation (including fishing, canoeing, kayaking, and greenways along its length).

The town of Seymour has gone through several name changes. Originally established as a part of Derby, Seymour was known as Naugatuck until 1738, after which it was known as Chusetown in honor of the Indian Chief Joseph Chuse.

Gen. David Humphreys, who fought alongside George Washington, was given the honor of having the town renamed Humphreysville in 1804. Humphreys was a key manufacturer, transforming Seymour into a manufacturing town by starting a woolen mill along the Naugatuck in 1806. Prior to this, he established the first paper mill in town in 1805.

In 1850, Seymour became incorporated as the 148th town in Connecticut with a population of 1,677. The name Seymour was chosen to honor the sitting governor, Thomas H. Seymour.

Several incidents have led to the changing of the downtown area of Seymour. During the 1800s to late 1900s, Seymour was known as a mill town. Many manufacturing businesses were located along the Naugatuck River, where the power was harnessed to run machinery. During those early days of manufacturing, Seymour was known to have the finest woolen mill, the Tingue Woolen Mills. In addition, Waterman Bic, now known as Bic, had its beginnings here in Seymour. Many residents are unaware of these local manufacturing start-ups, along with others, such as hoops for hoop skirts and the first machine-pointed horseshoe nails. Kerite Manufacturing, which is the oldest factory still in existence in Seymour, started in 1854. Kerite, with a history all its own, continues to make wiring and cable that is used worldwide.

The downtown area has changed several times over the years. On August 13, 1955, Hurricane Connie dropped 4–6 inches of rain. Five days later, 14 inches of rain fell in a 30-hour period. The flood of 1955 changed much of downtown as the Naugatuck River breached the area. President Dwight D. Eisenhower declared Connecticut a national disaster area due to the great loss of life and property. The construction of state highway Route 8 in the early 1960s also changed the landscape of Seymour.

Many landmarks from the past are no longer here. Roadways have changed. Roads have been added. This even makes a longtime resident stop to think about where points are on a map. In addition, dams that were there no longer are. The same is true with sluiceways that once provided water to power the factories.

The same changes that affected the landscape also carry through to other parts of the town. What was once the high school became the grammar school and changed once again to become privately owned offices. Such changes with school buildings are not unique. The location of the small schoolhouse known as Cedar Ridge is now Veterans Park on Pearl Street and a part of the Seymour Land Trust.

The scope of this book covers the early history of Seymour through the floods of 1955 and the period after the flood. A few pages are devoted to where Seymour is today with its changes. One focal point is the community pride and spirit that the town has at its core. The New England tradition of coming together for community events is one that the townspeople cherish.

As we move on through our lives, may we all continue to share the experiences and hand down a piece of our own history to enrich the lives of others following in our footsteps.

One

OUR EARLY HOMES

Probably the most historically significant building was known as the Turel Whittemore Tavern, which was constructed around 1740. Turel Whittemore purchased the property in 1778. The second story was added in 1867 by Martin Castle. It was here that the infamous Dayton Robbery was plotted by a British officer during the Revolutionary era in 1780. The building, located at 114 South Main Street, has housed various businesses over the years, including restaurants and, most recently, an ice cream shop. (Marian K. O'Keefe.)

The Dayton Tavern at 121 South Main Street was built prior to 1780. Capt. Ebenezer Dayton was a privateersman who antagonized the Tories on Long Island Sound during the Revolutionary era. It was at this time that the robbery of his home in Bethany occurred after the plotting at the Whittemore Tavern. After the war, he moved to Seymour, where he kept the inn, which, ironically, was located opposite the Whittemore Tavern. At one time, Gen. David Humphreys boarded here. The home continues to be used as a private residence. (Marian K. O'Keefe.)

The Stiles/Stoddard House at 3-5 Pearl Street stands on the site of a home originally built by Indian Chief Chuse, who moved from the falls on the Naugatuck River to be a neighbor to the white people. In 1795, Nathaniel Stiles built this home, which still stands today. He married Phoebe, the daughter of Capt. Ebenezer Dayton. Dr. Abiram Stoddard moved into this home in the early 1800s and was the second local physician for the town. Dr. Stoddard also was a representative to the General Assembly in 1814. (Marian K. O'Keefe.)

In the period around 1700, Henry Wooster settled in Seymour. He built his home on 150 acres 1 mile south of the falls on the east side of the river. The house stands today at 387 South Main Street. The home was handed down to five generations of Henrys. The widow of the last Henry married Capt. Daniel Moss, whose name was used for the adjacent street. (Marian K. O'Keefe.)

Elbow Room Farm, located at 179 Great Hill Road, was built around 1750–1800. The most famous owner was Col. John Bakeless, an author and historian. He lived here from 1940 to 1970. He wrote vivid accounts of espionage during the Revolutionary War, including *Turncoat, Traitors and Heroes*. He also served as an intelligence agent during World War II and was a professor at Columbia University. Dr. Bakeless claimed that the house was haunted by a woman who told her niece to wear red flannel underwear. (Marian K. O'Keefe.)

The private residence of Ephraim Smith was built at 318 Roosevelt Drive in 1757. The home was built in the saltbox style with a center stone chimney. For many years, it was used as an inn and stagecoach stop on the route from Albany. The inside steps at this entrance show evidence that many a keg of "cider" was rolled through the door. (Marian K. O'Keefe.)

The Bassett/Healy Homestead, also known as Balance Rock Farm, is located at 58 Bungay Road. It is a Colonial-style home that was built in 1776. The name of the farm was taken from a huge rock formation that is now on the property of the Balance Rock condominium complex. The first owner of this home was Abner Tibbals, who was a teacher and a farmer. (Marian K. O'Keefe.)

Daniel Holbrook built this house for his son, Col. Daniel Holbrook, in 1780 at 112 Skokorat Street. Col. Holbrook was in the 2nd Regiment of the militia. According to *Seymour Past and Present*, when one approaches in the evening, "one might think the grove a good place for the witches to frolic." The home was later sold to Joel and Ruth Chatfield. (Marian K. O'Keefe.)

Located on the highest point of the Great Hill section of Seymour at 79 Great Hill Road, the Priest Abner Smith home was built in 1788 in the gambrel style. Reverend Smith was the pastor of the Great Hill Society Church in 1786. He served as pastor until 1829. It later became the Bomba Dairy Farm, which has been in operation since 1912. The state has recently purchased the development rights to the property so that it will continue to remain farmland. (Marian K. O'Keefe.)

The oldest section of this house in the rear was built by Dr. Samuel Sanford, who was Seymour's first physician in 1793. Dr. Sanford established a smallpox hospital near Castle Rock in 1797. The front section was probably built by Gen. David Humphrey. His nephew, Judge John Humphrey, lived here in the 1820s. He and his brother William had charge of the Humphrey Woolen Mill. The home is located at 63–65 West Street. (Marian K. O'Keefe.)

Ann S. Stephens was born in this 18th-century cottage located at 153 West Street in 1810. Stephens was thought to have written the first dime novels. She wrote about 30 novels over her career. Her book *The Gold Brick* was set among the localities of what was then Humphreysville, and she used some characters who lived in the town. Stevens died on August 20, 1886, in Newport, Rhode Island. (Marian K. O'Keefe.)

The home of the Honorable Carlos French is no longer standing. He was born in Seymour on August 6, 1835, and attended common schools in the town and then a New Haven military school. French was credited with inventing the spiral steel car spring. His legacy remains in his donation of 14 acres, now known as French Memorial Park, to the townspeople of Seymour. He died in 1903. (Barton Collection.)

Seymour, Connecticut · 1870

This drawing depicts Seymour in 1870 with the falls area of the Naugatuck River still the center of town and its businesses and industry. The population had risen to 2,121 by this time. Located at the falls and on the right side of the Naugatuck River are the Tingue Manufacturing Company and the New Haven Copper Company. Clustered around the river and Broad Street in the falls area were many small businesses and homes.

James Swan was born in Dumfries, Scotland, on December 18, 1833, where, according to *Seymour Past and Present*, he was "reared in an atmosphere of religion and of patriotism." He is credited with over 70 patents for tools and manufacturing processes. Swan was a leader in the community, both in the Congregational church and the library. He was president of the James Swan Company and the H. A. Matthews Manufacturing Company located on River Street at what is now known as the Housatonic Wire Company.

This Victorian-style home was built in 1881 for James Swan, a leading Seymour manufacturer. Swan married Miss Agnes Bell in 1857 and raised one daughter and three sons. Even now, the home has had few changes. Its location is at 276 Bank Street, where it houses professional office space. (Marian K. O'Keefe.)

This beautiful home stands on 28 Pearl Street and was known as the Davis-Wooster House. The home was constructed in 1851 in the Queen Anne/vernacular style of building. The original owner was Isaac Davis. Letsome Wooster, brother of H. H. H. Wooster and superintendent of the Seymour Specialty Company, lived here in the last part of the 19th century. (Marian K. O'Keefe.)

This vernacular-style farmhouse was built in 1881 at 130 Skokorat Street. The porch was added to the original home later. This was the farmhouse of Paul and Rose Chatfield, for whom the Paul E. Chatfield School is named. It was sold to the current owners, Francis and Anna Conroy, upon the death of Mrs. Chatfield.

The home of Dr. Frank A. Benedict was built in 1894 at 27 Washington Avenue. The tower has been removed from the original home. Dr. Benedict graduated from Yale in 1887 with a medical degree and moved to Seymour in 1892. As well as practicing medicine, he was the health officer of the town, a member of the 2nd Company of the Governor's Horse Guards, and a member of the Citizens Engine Company. (Marian K. O'Keefe.)

This Queen Ann structure was built in 1879 and was home to one of Connecticut's leading industrialists, William Henry Harrison Wooster, founder of the Seymour Manufacturing Company, The Seymour Water Company, and the Seymour Trust. Legend has it that the last descendent of Wooster's (Ruth) still occupies the home and that her ghost can be seen from time to time. The building stands at 153 North Street. (Marian K. O'Keefe.)

The Austin Goodyear Day House was constructed in a Victorian Gothic–Queen Anne style in 1885. Day's most famous product was Kerite, which is used for telegraph, fire alarms, and power cables. Kerite's is the oldest continuously operated wire and cable company in the United States. Located at 44 Day Street, the building has been restored and is in use by the company. (Marian K. O'Keefe.)

The Andrew Y. Beach residence was built in 1886 at 12 Bank Street. Beach worked for the Hartford and New Haven Railroad, where he was a station agent for Naugatuck and Seymour, a general ticket agent of Bridgeport, and a general agent of Springfield, Massachusetts. After spending 14 years in Springfield, he returned to Seymour in 1886, building his home at 12 Bank Street. The home has been renovated and houses the law offices of May and Kulas. (Barton Collection.)

The Charles H. Lounsbury Store is a building reminiscent of a bygone era. The structure is located at 42–44 Maple Street, across from the Anna LoPresti School. In the late 1800s, Charles Lounsbury was proprietor of the general store. His stock included dry goods, boots, and shoes, as well as grain and feed. Lounsbury represented Beacon Falls in the General Assembly, and while a resident of Seymour, he was elected to the Board of Selectmen. (Barton Collection.)

This home at 59 West Street was built in 1940 as the private residence of Katharine Matthies, daughter of Seymour industrialist George Matthies. Miss Matthies was known for her philanthropy, supporting many community groups. She resided in the home until she died in 1987 at age 85. In 1995, the Seymour Historical Society assumed ownership and responsibility of the Matthies house as its permanent home. (Marian K. O'Keefe.)

Two

THE WORK THAT
IDENTIFIED SEYMOUR

First Woolen Mill in U. S., Seymour, Conn.
Erected by Gen, David Humphrey, 1804,

The first woolen mill in the United States was established by Gen. David Humphreys in 1804. Humphreys was born in Derby. He was educated at Yale, graduating at 19 years of age with honors. Humphreys was in the Revolutionary War, where he saw battle and was appointed aide-de-camp to George Washington in 1780. The town was named Humphreysville for 50 years to honor the poet, warrior, statesman, and manufacturer.

SEYMOUR AS IT WAS IN 1812

Displaying the banner "Humphreysville," the town is depicted in this woodcut made for use as a trademark by the paper mill. The large building to the right of the saw mill was the woolen factory in which David Humphreys made the first broadcloth ever manufactured in the United States. The wool used was from merino sheep that he brought back from Spain when he was ambassador there after the war.

This blacksmith shop was located at the intersection of Pearl and Maple Streets. The building was made of stone and wood with a brick chimney. The owner was recorded as Edwin or Edmund Page in 1798. During the late 1800s it became the site for Walter French's manufacturing of augers.

HUMPHREYSVILLE.

JAM NOVA PROGENES.

PERSEVERANDO.

{ SHIELD }
{ WITH VINES. }

PACTA SEMPER SERVANDA.

MDCCCX.

This silk flag was beautifully embroidered by Lady Humphreys and was in the possession of Carlos French, Esq. The reverse side had a semicircle of 16 stars, "Humphreys Ville," an eagle, arrows, and state emblems.

Rail was an important part of the activity for the citizens and manufacturers during the late 1800s. On the hand truck and stored to the left are small wooden Kerite wire wheels. Inside the freight station, the names of the workers are listed as follows: ? Philbrock, John Geutti, John Weymer, Wilbur Doolittle, unidentified, and Eugene Clark. (Citizens Engine Company No. 2.)

Chinese laundries were commonplace in the United States during the beginning of the 20th century. In 1902, Jun Sing operated the laundry on Bank Street, opposite Third Street. To the left of the laundry was the east entrance to the wooden bridge over the Naugatuck River. On the right side was McNerny's Blacksmith Shop. Willie McNerny was also the town constable. Long before radar was in use, McNerny was able to know if a horse was travelling too fast over the wooden bridge by the gallop of the horse's hooves. He would rush out and grab the reins and reprimand the rider.

This advertisement in 1902 for the "Works of James Swan" listed all the different tools that the manufacturer produced. It also provides an artist's rendition of what the business looked like at the time.

This photograph, taken in 1895 by E. S. Cooper, shows factory workers at the Swan Shop located on Bank Street posing for a picture. Shown are ? Geschimsky, Otto Geschimsky, Fred Fox, Pat Vaughn, Will Hubbell, Edar Miller, L. L. Garrett, Grant Hubbell, William Miles, E. C. Greywacz, Sam Beach, J. A. Griffith, Herman Wirth, William Dempsky, Gus Dempsky, William Foster, George Liester Jr., Walter Dorman, Theodore Adams, George Wyant, Howard Riggs, Charles Wheeler, George Lester Sr., Fred Northrop, Emery Adams, John Riggs, Andrew Schuster, Wilson Wyant, Joseph Foster, and Richard Pearson.

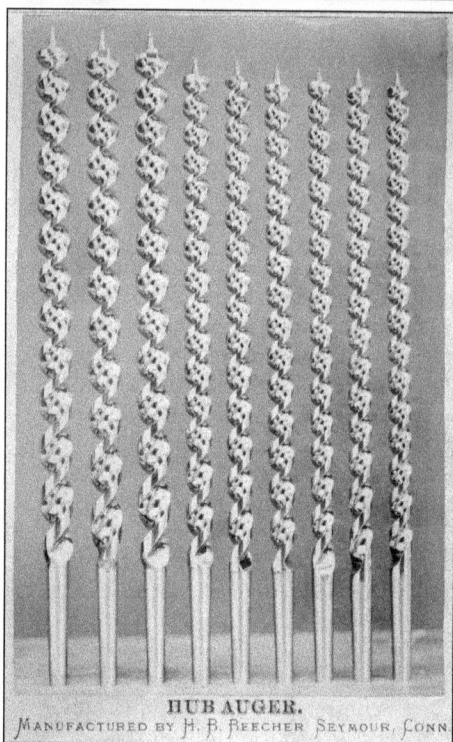

HUB AUGER.
MANUFACTURED BY H. B. BEECHER SEYMOUR, CONN.

This building, located about a third of a mile from the Naugatuck River on Little River, became H. B. Beecher's Mill until the death of Beecher in 1880. His son, Frank Henry Beecher, carried on the family business of manufacturing augers and bits. The factory was situated at a falls, where the water was used for power. (Barton Collection.)

One of six partners who originally made up the manufacturing business of French, Swift and Company in 1847 was Henry Beers Beecher. In 1866, he became the sole owner and the last survivor of the firm. Pictured here is a collection of the many augers and bits that he manufactured. (Richard Joy.)

The Humphreysville Manufacturing Company was started in 1806. Its principal line of manufacturing was augers and bits. There were several buildings on the site, including the main building, office and shipping department, and the forging rooms. The goods were known for their excellent material and workmanship. Along the factory was the sluiceway that channeled the water for power. (Barton Collection.)

The Seymour Electric Light Company was incorporated in 1889. It was located next to the Naugatuck River on Main Street across from Day Street. The company had the contract for town lighting, along with furnishing arc or incandescent lighting to manufacturers and residences. It has been said that residents on the outskirts of downtown knew when a good card game was in progress under the bridge because someone would go up to the electric company and pay them extra money to keep the lights on. (Jarvis Collection.)

This 1902 Seymour Electric company bill was to the Nonnawauk Tribe #9 I.O.R.M. (Improved Order of Red Men). The group held its meetings in a hall on Main Street in the Davis block.

The Arethusa Spring Water Company was organized in 1892 by Carlos French, who had tested the purity of the water coming from the spring on Walnut Hill. The water company was located on Pearl Street in the vicinity of Great Oak. The water was bottled as both sparkling and clear. It was labeled the "purest spring water known." The laboratories of the company were models of cleanliness and aimed to provide water free from all pollutants. It was also reported that people, including doctors, felt that the water would promote health and even cure diseases. In the winter scene below, the white tower to the right of the building is the fountain when it froze. (Barton Collection.)

Located on the corner of Main and Bank Streets where Rogol's block now stands, the Valley National Bank was organized on August 14, 1900. In 1904, it was dissolved and gave way to The Seymour Trust Company. As with today's practice of bank changes, the changeover was fairly smooth, without the majority of customers noticing any interruptions. (Barton Collection.)

On October 26, 1923, the Seymour Trust Company opened a new bank on Main Street as one of the most up-to-date banks in the state. The bank prided itself on its vaults from the Mosler Safe Company, as well as Mosler delayed time locks and the federal tear gas system, which could be used in the event of a holdup. The current bank at this location on Main Street is Bank of America. (Marian K. O'Keefe.)

The E. C. Sharpe Building and Lumber Company was incorporated in May 1898, with E. C. Sharpe as president. The business serviced local builders and residents with lumber, laths, timber, and other assorted building materials. Located at 1 Main Street adjoining the railroad tracks, it was known to have the best of shipping and receiving facilities. (Barton Collection.)

The *Record* was established in 1871 as the first newspaper to be published between Derby and Waterbury. The *Record* was conducted by William C. Sharpe, who went on to publish Seymour's history in 1902 with the book *Seymour Past and Present*. He was instrumental in preserving Seymour's early history, both in his newspaper and books. The *Record* was published by Sharpe until his death and then by others until the mid-1940s. The building was located at 72 Main Street. (Barton Collection.)

O. D. Sykes operated his plumbing business out of this storefront on Main Street. He was reputed to complete fine work that was demanded by the rigorous laws for this type of work. He was known to take care with his work to ensure proper ventilation and drainage. In addition, his store carried a large stock of stoves, ranges, furnaces, and lamps. (Barton Collection.)

The Samuel R. Dean Store was located at 43–45 Main Street and was founded in 1850. Upon the death of Dean, his wife Anna took over the store with her son Robert as general manager. The store was designated as the best general store in the area, carrying a varied assortment of dry goods, groceries, hardware, paints, and oils. (Barton Collection.)

In 1902, Thomas J. Thomas became the sole proprietor of this store on Main Street. He had originally partnered with L. K. Holmes to begin the grocery trade in January of 1893. According to *The Seymour Record*, the store provided "fancy and staple groceries of every description." Thomas had two delivery teams on the road and employed five assistants. (Barton Collection.)

This building on Main Street was home to two businesses in the early 1900s. The post office occupied the space on the right, while the Seymour Pharmacy occupied the left. The sign on the outside advertises "Stuart's Dyspepsia Tablets for Sour Stomach Indigestion." (Barton Collection.)

Described as a department store, the store of Andrew Y. Beach bears little resemblance to today's department stores. Beach was described as an energetic and thoughtful businessman who could meet the demands of the people. The store was established in 1887 and was located at 13 Main Street. The sign advertised coal, grain, and flour; however, it has been recorded that it was a "pure food" store that could be relied upon for the best quality foods. To the right was the People's Market, a fine meat store that also advertised as a "cash market." (Barton Collection.)

In 1902, the Independent Order of Odd Fellows building was completed at 151 Main Street. The group was instituted on May 21, 1851, with 13 charter members. It was known in 1877 for its large lodge library of over 700 books. The organization's work included caring for the sick and providing benefits to widows and the fatherless. (Barton Collection.)

By the early 1900s, most homes and businesses were equipped for refrigeration with an icebox. This early precursor of the modern refrigerator used frozen blocks of ice that were harvested during the winter and stored in the icehouse using sawdust as insulation. This photograph shows ice being harvested at Silver Lake off North Street and conveyed to the icehouse on the lower right. Rimmon Rock is the large hill on the upper left. (Barton Collection.)

1914
SEYMOUR MFG. CASTING SHOP

R TO L H. HUMMEL - SPAKOWSKI - SEPANEK - TONY BOLOVI
W. HUMMEL

The men of the Seymour Manufacturing Casting Shop take a moment to pose for a picture. This photograph gives a good idea of what it was like to work in one of the factories at the beginning of the century. Worker safety standards were not established until 56 years later, when the Occupational and Safety Act of 1970 was enacted to protect workers. Shown from left to right are H. Hummel, ? Spakowski, ? Sepanek, Tony Bolovic, and W. Hummel. (Citizens Engine Company No. 2.)

This site along the falls of the Naugatuck River was first the home of a sawmill in the 1700s. It changed hands many times until General Humphreys erected factories for the manufacture of woolen cloth. In 1880, John H. Tingue purchased the property and organized the Tingue Manufacturing Company. The principal product of these mills was plush, which was known to be the best on the market. Charles Coupland, the general manager, invented a new and very speedy way of weaving mohair pile goods into mohair plush using the fleece of the Angora goat. The postcard below shows the mill with the Waterman building. (Richard Joy, Fred Watton.)

TINGUE SILK MILLS AND WATERMAN FOUNTAIN PEN FACTORY, SEYMOUR, CONN.

The last of the H. P. and E. Day Pen Company's early buildings is shown here along the bank of the Naugatuck River near the falls. Directly behind the building is the New Haven Copper Company, and to the left is the new apartment building that replaced the Waterman Bic building. H. P. and E. Day manufactured vulcanized hard rubber goods, including fountain pens and propelling pencils and penholders. The nephews of Charles Goodyear, Henry P. and Edmund Day developed a process for cleaning and sheeting rubber so that it could be used to better advantage by another local business, the Kerite Insulated Cable Company, which was owned by their brother, Austin G. Day. In 1946, the Waterman Company purchased the manufacturing assets of H. P. and E. Day, Inc. (Marian K. O'Keefe.)

The Rimmon Manufacturing Company was incorporated on January 10, 1900. The company made shoe and corset eyelets and other metal goods. The company was located on Day Street by Main Street. The president of the company was George Matthies, who was also the assistant treasurer of the Seymour Manufacturing Company. (Barton Collection.)

Papermaking was a thriving business in Seymour. In 1850, Sharon Y. Beach established the Seymour Paper Mills on a site along Bladen's Brook, which is now Beach Street. The mill produced various grades of paper needed for wrapping, newspapers, magazines, and other specialties. Owners changed several times over the years until the final ownership, which manufactured facial and toilet tissue. People still remember knowing the color of the paper being made that day by the color of the brook. (Barton Collection.)

In 1895, this American Tea and Coffee wagon made its rounds in downtown Seymour. Although little information can be found on this wagon, the image illustrates the two drinks' long-standing popularity with Americans.

The W. D. Ingersoll store at 39 Main Street was a clothing store established in 1888. The store advertised that "good taste in dressing is an evidence of good breeding." Ingersoll stocked clothing of excellent quality and texture and did an extensive business in custom tailoring. He was a native of New York before moving to Seymour. (Barton Collection.)

In 1871, George Smith purchased the People's Drug Store from Dr. Henry Davis. His stock included an extensive supply of drugs intended to combat all the "ills that flesh is heir to." This sense of security gave people a reason to deal with Smith. He also stocked toilet goods, fine perfumery, stationery, and cigars. He was active in the community as a member of the Masons, Knights of Pythias, and Red Men, as well as being a charter member of the Citizens Engine Company. (Barton Collection.)

A receipt from George Smith, the proprietor of the People's Drug Store, records the purchase of 50 cigars in the amount of $2 to the Nonnewauk Tribe on March 1, 1909.

The Seymour Commercial Company was located on Main Street. The company provided residents with sporting goods, ammunition, radios, and tires. There was also a gas pump on the far right. Shown from left to right are Fritz Hummel, George Woodward, Mildred Stocking, and Frank Warr. (Citizens Engine Company No. 2.)

This store was established by E. F. Bassett in 1855 on Bank Street. In 1889, W. L. Ward became the proprietor. The store had a good reputation for its fine home furnishings. Ward was also a director of funerals, later merging into the present Miller-Ward Funeral Home. The store and its wares would still be in fashion today in Seymour's antique district. (Citizens Engine Company No. 2.)

William R. Brixey came to America from England in 1879 and located in Seymour. In 1892, he became the sole owner of the Kerite Insulated Wire and Cable Works. Brixey increased the size of the plant in order to expedite large orders. His exhibit at the Worlds' Fair earned him medals and awards for the high grade of insulated wires and cables that the company produced. (Barton Collection.)

Charles Mitchell, a German immigrant, was one of the many immigrants who found gainful employment in Seymour. The machine feeding wire into cable in this photograph from the 1940s is still in use today for producing cable that is used worldwide, including for use in oil drilling.

A family stops to pose for a photograph in the Seymour Candy Company at 116 Main Street in this 1920s–1930s picture. The store sold many confections, from handmade chocolates in the left cases to Beech-Nut candy and gums at the front on the right. The milkshake mixer on the counter stands ready for other treats to be made. (Alex Danka.)

The Joseph W. Foster Barber Shop was located on Main Street to the right of the wooden stairs that crossed the railroad tracks. The traditional barber pole is located outside on the sidewalk in its familiar striped pattern. The house in the background is located on Humphrey Street. (Citizens Engine Company No. 2.)

When people in Seymour remember the Silver Grill, they think of "Big Mike." Mike and Stella Ostaszeski moved to Seymour in the late 1920s during the height of the Depression. In 1936, they opened this popular restaurant across the street from the New Haven Copper Company on Main Street. The Seymour Alumni Club was located above the restaurant. The Ostaszeskis continued with several other restaurant ventures in the area. (James Zepos.)

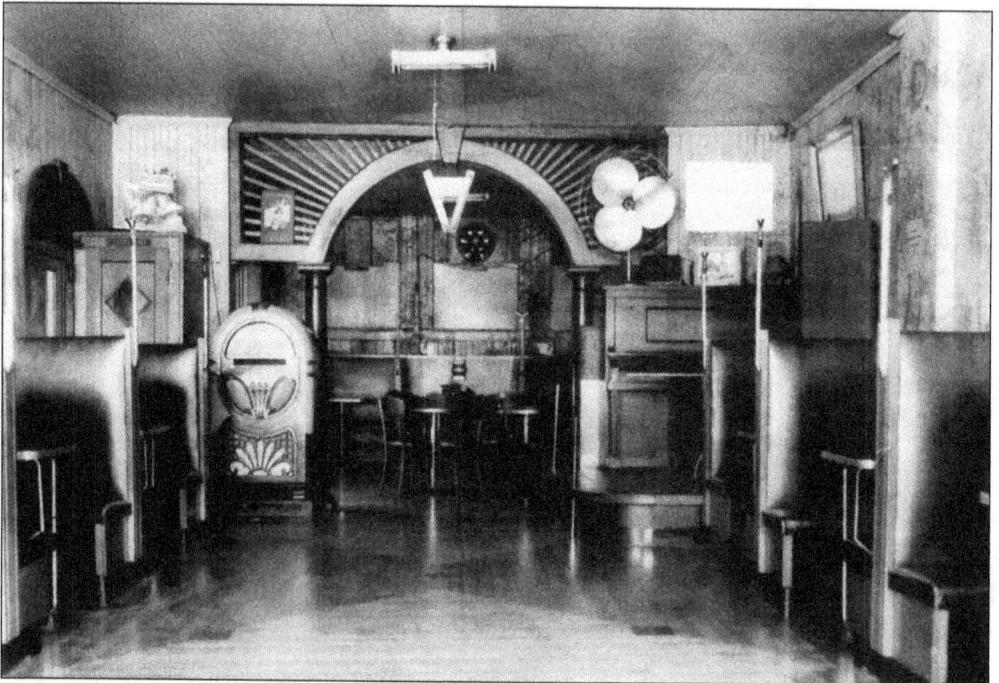

Mac's grocery and liquor stores were conveniently located along Broad Street. The window displays in both stores proudly exhibit the wares for sale. The area was once populated with more homes in the downtown area prior to the flood of 1955.

In 1950, Frank and Ralph Ajello pose for a picture while loading the milk truck for delivery. Milk was sold in glass quart bottles with a cardboard seal. The dairy farm was located in the Great Hill section of town and continued to be one of the largest dairy farms. Parts of the farm later became the Great Hill Country Club, now Great Hill Estates. (Frank Ajello.)

Three

THE LANDSCAPES THAT WERE HERE

Bank Street in downtown Seymour continues to look much the same as it did in 1902. To the right is First Street and on the left, Columbus Street. At the corner is a sign for Mrs. E. Taylor, dry goods and millinery, while the upper corner of the building displays a sign for a dentist. Directly at the end of Bank Street is the wooden covered bridge. (Barton Collection.)

This view of Main Street looking north in 1902 shows a bustling downtown area, with wagons traveling the well-worn dirt road. The Samuel Dean store is on the left with several people standing in front. The railroad station on the right was a busy area. (Barton Collection.)

The trolley tracks in upper Main Street tell of a bygone era. The trolley was a means of travel from Waterbury and through the valley to New Haven. Both homes and businesses once populated this area. (Jarvis Collection.)

TROLLEY CAR wrecked at Seymour, Conn., Dec. 26, 1909, down 50ft bank into Rimon Pond. Photo taken directly after accident, while crew were still in car. Photo by Geo. Ford, Seymour, Conn.

On December 26, 1909, at the height of a blizzard, an inbound trolley from Waterbury jumped the rails just south of the Rimmon switch, smashed through the guardrail, and plunged 40 feet down a steep embankment into 18 feet of water at Rimmon Pond. The motorman and conductor were trapped underwater in the vestibule and drowned, but the five passengers escaped. The only witness to the accident was a girl who saw it from the upper window of a house on Meadow Street. (Fred Watton.)

This busy railroad line was used for both passengers and freight. The downtown depot area shows how busy it could be, with five rail lines at the station in 1902. The three-story building on the right was the Webster Hotel, which provided overnight accommodations to travelers and rail crew. (Barton Collection.)

NAUGATUCK RAILROAD.

TRAINS RUN AS FOLLOWS.

LEAVE SEYMOUR.   GOING NORTH.

6.49 A. M., Extra Freight, with Passenger Car.
8.55 A. M., Milk Train for Winsted.
10.54 A. M., Passenger Train for Winsted.
12.40 P. M., Freight Train for Winsted.
4.17 P. M., Freight Train with Passenger Car attached for Waterbury.
5.44 P. M., Passenger Train for Winsted.
8-11 P. M., Special for Waterbury.
9.44 A. M., Sunday, for Winsted.

LEAVE SEYMOUR.   GOING SOUTH.

5.50 A. M., Freight Train with Passenger Car attached, for Bridgeport and N. Y.
8.55 A. M.. Express Train for Bridgeport, New York and New Haven, (through cars.)
11.05 A. M., Freight Train for Bridgeport.
12.40 P. M,, Special for Bridgeport, New York and New Haven.
3.04 P. M., Passenger Train for Bridgeport, New York and New Haven.
7.08 P. M., Milk Train connecting at Bridgeport with Express for New York.
6.02 P. M., Sunday, Milk Train for Bridgeport.

T. B. BEACH, Agent.
GEO. W. BEACH, Superintendent.

The first railroad from Bridgeport to Seymour was opened in 1849. This Naugatuck Railroad train schedule from the start of the 20th century shows how frequent train service was during this time. Milk was an important agricultural item that needed to travel to the cities. George W. Beach was supervisor for the railroad.

Both part of the charm and part of the infrastructure, this wooden stairway provided a means for residents of the Humphreys Street area to safely cross over the railroad to Main Street. Many photographs from this period around 1900 bear the acknowledgement of the local pharmacist, George Smith. (Jarvis Collection.)

This scenic view looking from French Memorial Park accents the railroad bridges, one steel and one covered bridge, across the span of the Naugatuck River. Behind the bridges, the downtown area can be seen with its many homes and businesses. In the far distance, behind the smokestack, the covered bridge spans the river. (Barton Collection.)

A key infrastructure as important to the town as the river was the railroad. Centrally located on Main Street, this impressive view depicts the steam locomotive at the station heading from Waterbury towards Bridgeport. The station was built in 1889. Horse and carriage was the only other means of transportation at this time. The two large smokestacks appearing behind the station were across the river at the Seymour Manufacturing Company. (Barton Collection.)

The entrance to the covered bridge was captured in this photograph by William C. Bryant of New York City around 1900. He was known as an artistic photographer who spent many summers photographing Seymour and surrounding areas. William C. Sharpe, author of *Seymour Past and Present*, was indebted to him for many of the photographs that were used in his book. To the right is a billboard displaying upcoming events. Gas lamps were used to light the streets.

This covered wooden bridge spanned the Naugatuck River on Bank Street. Bridges were an important part of the industrial center. When Seymour was incorporated in 1850, the town leaders voted to undertake the repair of its bridges. During this time, many floods caused damage to the bridges. In 1856, this bridge was built at the west end of Bank Street. The covered area with lattice work was for pedestrian crossing. The bridge was removed in 1936 to make way for the new concrete bridge. (Steven Pupchyk.)

The paper mill pond at the juncture of Beach Street and Route 67 was once an expansive, open pond. It was an attraction for families during the winter months when it was frozen over and ideal for ice skating. The roadway on the left is Skokorat Street. The Indian name *Scucurra* meant Snake Hill. Many residents can attest to that fact, as many snakes, mostly harmless, still populate the area. The white house on the right was home to Rev. Sylvester Smith, for whom the street was named. (Barton Collection.)

In this view from French Memorial Park looking west, the Seymour Manufacturing Company's smoke stacks tower over the Naugatuck River, which flows over the Rimmon Dam. To the left, North Main is shown in the location of Route 8. At this time, there were no state roads traversing the landscape. (Barton Collection.)

Prior to the 1955 flood, downtown Seymour had homes and businesses located on what were known as First, Second, and Third Streets. Third Street met up with Bank Street at the beginning of the wooden bridge on the east side of the river. This area was home to many of the local saloons that factory workers patronized at the end of their shifts. After the flood, the area was used for the construction of Route 8 and town parking. (Jarvis Collection.)

The junction of River and West Streets was always a major throughway from the west side of town. Although both roadways were made of dirt, West Street had a finished sidewalk made of cement. In the far distance is an unobstructed view of Center School. (Barton Collection.)

Taken from Castle Rock, this photograph gives an overview of the downtown area. The area that was once heavily populated was in the center, where the dark green pine trees stand. The area was known as Pine Street and was home to local businesses and residents. On the hill to the right stands St. Augustine Church, while in the middle stands the Congregational church. (Barton Collection.)

On October 16, 1889, a grand parade was given by the Citizens Engine Company, which hosted seven visiting fire companies. The town draped itself in decorations for the festivities that ended with a banquet in large tents on the firehouse grounds. This photograph of the parade was taken from the west side of the Broad Street bridge. (Barton Collection.)

The buildings shown in this picture are a part of the Humphreys building, also known as the Casagrande building. This offices of the Fowler Nail Company (organized in 1866) were here. The company produced the first satisfactory machine-pointed horseshoe nails. (Barton Collection.)

The home in the center at the corner of DeForest and First Streets stands on the location of what would later become Seymour Town Hall. Along DeForest Street stood homes that would, in later years, be demolished to make room for the expansion of the Citizens Engine Company. (Citizens Engine Company No. 2.)

In 1847, the wooden dam about a quarter mile above the falls was replaced with a solid masonry dam constructed by Raymond French. The overflow was about 300 feet long and the fall about 19 feet. The dam was used to furnish power downstream for the Fowler Nail Company, the Seymour Manufacturing Company, and the Electric Light Company. (Richard Joy.)

On Memorial Day in 1933, soldiers and firemen march in the parade on Main Street near Route 67. The Strand parking lot to the right was at a higher elevation and sported billboards both on the side of the building and in the parking lot. (Citizens Engine Company No. 2.)

The Broad Street bridge area has seen many changes since this photograph from around 1900. Looking down on the steel Broad Street bridge from Humphrey Street, many homes and businesses can be seen. They would later be destroyed by the floods. On the bottom right corner still stands the Trestle Tavern. (Barton Collection.)

12/28/1947
FRONT OF NEW HAVEN COPPER CO
MAIN ST.
DONATED BY ART YOUNG

The unexpected blizzard of December 27, 1947, brought almost 2 feet of snow to New York and several inches to the area in less than 24 hours. A casualty of the storm was a freight car that jumped the tracks across from the New Haven Copper Company. (Citizens Engine Company No. 2.)

EFFECTIVE NOVEMBER 26, 1949

MID-WEEK

Tues.-Wed.-Thurs.

EXCURSION

WATERBURY Bridgeport
Naugatuck
$1.15 ROUND TRIP

SEYMOUR Bridgeport
Beacon Falls
$.86 ROUND TRIP

ANSONIA
DERBY $.50 ROUND TRIP
SHELTON

SAVE

BY USING
LOW RATE, 12-RIDE
COMMUTATION TICKETS

Inquire of Your Local Ticket Agent

★ **NEW YORK** ★

Direct Train Connections
at Bridgeport

HARTFORD
Direct Bus Connections
AT WATERBURY

Packages sent by Intercity
save Time and Money

AGENTS

Bridgeport — Greyhound Terminal
77 Plaza   Tel. 4-4185
Quaker City Bus Depot
56 Golden Hill St.   Tel. 6-2525
Shelton — Kyle's Stationery Store
Tel. 3490
Derby — Harding Pharmacy
Tel. 1177
Ansonia (W.S.) — Lears Pharmacy
Tel. 1113
Seymour — Carroll's Cut-Rate
143 Main St.   Tel. 2824
Beacon Falls — O'Connell's
Tel. Naug. 4991
Naugatuck — Naugatuck Pharmacy
Tel. 4288
Waterbury Bus Depot, 24 Bank St.
Tel. 3-5032

Office
4490 Main Street, Bridgeport
Telephone 6-3558

The Intercity Valley Line
Greyhound Feeder Line

WATERBURY
UNION CITY
NAUGATUCK
BEACON FALLS
SEYMOUR
ANSONIA W. S.
DERBY-SHELTON
NICHOLS
BRIDGEPORT

Direct Connections at
WATERBURY for HARTFORD
BRISTOL — NEW BRITAIN
PLAINVILLE

Connections at Bridgeport for

NEW YORK
FREQUENT TRAINS

GREYHOUND
TICKET AGENTS
"Coast to Coast"

This Greyhound bus schedule from 1949 gives departure times for both northbound travel to Winsted and southbound travel to New York. The bus was an important means of transportation in addition to the railroad and automobiles.

This bird's-eye view from the top of French Memorial Park shows the downtown landscape. Another important mode of transportation was the trolley. The trolley began operation in 1901 from Ansonia to Seymour and later was extended to Waterbury. The last trolley went through Seymour on June 19, 1937. Seen here, a trolley is making its way south from Beacon Falls.

Seymour men and women have always participated in the wars in which the United States has engaged. This monument that looks out over the town from French Memorial Park was erected in honor and gratitude to those who took part in the Civil War. The town sent 128 men to the war that was also known as The War for the Preservation of the Union. (Marian K. O'Keefe.)

The iron Broad Street bridge was a second crossing over the Naugatuck River that was built in 1883. The Seymour House, a local hotel, was on the left, while Mac's grocery and liquor store was on the opposite side of the road. In the background, the Tingue plush mill is seen, along with the tall Waterman-Bic building on the right. (John Felenchak.)

The flood of 1955 destroyed the area that was once a thriving business section of Seymour. This view shows a gas station/car dealer to the right and Mac's liquor store and market. The new bridge area was expanded, taking away much of the location.

The year 1962 brought a new state highway through the region. Although the highway expedited travel, many residents felt that it destroyed the center of town, as it was elevated over the town and blocked many views, including Tingue Falls. (Marian K. O'Keefe.)

Four

PUBLIC GATHERING PLACES

In February 1797, Trinity Episcopal Church was organized as the then Union church on Church Street. Many changes have occurred to the building over the years, with the most recent renovation being done in 1997 when the church celebrated its 200th anniversary. The history from 1935 states that the church had probably held the record for the most lightning strikes of any other church in the state. This may have been because of its location and tall spire. The church is located at 91 Church Street. (Barton Collection.)

True to the heritage of Puritans and the pilgrims, the oldest church was the Seymour Congregational church built in 1789. The original site was later sold to the Methodist church in 1818. Due to the large congregation, the current church was built in 1846 and enlarged in 1890 on the corner of Broad Street and Derby Avenue. In keeping with its foundation of fellowship, Swan Memorial Hall was added in 1907 to accommodate the various parish activities. The church buildings needed extensive repairs after the floods of 1955. (Jarvis collection.)

In 1818, the Methodist Society purchased the first building in Seymour that was erected as a place of worship from the Congregationalist. The present building was erected as a new church in 1891 on Pearl Street. A fire destroyed much of the building in 2006 but it has since been repaired. (Barton Collection.)

The history of the Great Hill United Methodist Church goes back to the late 1700s. Preacher Jesse Lee, a circuit rider, was the first documented preacher, although others had come before him. The church, which was built in 1853–1854, is located on Great Hill Road south of the rotary intersection. (Marian K. O'Keefe.)

The first Catholic services were held in what is now the site of the Citizens Engine Company on DeForest Street. The cornerstone for St. Augustine's Roman Catholic Church was laid on July 15, 1888, on Washington Avenue. It was completed in time for Christmas services on December 25, 1889. In 1936, renovations covered the wood siding, shown in this picture, with brick. In 1966, a second Roman Catholic church, the Church of the Good Shepherd, was built in the Great Hill section on Mountain Road to accommodate the growing population of parishioners. (Barton Collection.)

The German Lutheran church, later known as the Immanuel Lutheran church, was organized in 1893. The site was selected on West Street, near Church Street and was dedicated on Thanksgiving Day in 1894. The Valley detachment of the Marine Corps League purchased the property in the 1970s and still maintains the building. Today, space is leased out for services by the Seymour Foursquare Church. (Jarvis collection.)

The first meeting of the Morning Star Lodge, No. 47, Free and Accepted Masons (the oldest fraternal organization in Seymour) was held on June 18, 1851. In 1901, the lodge was moved to the new Masonic hall in the Yale-Beach building. At the time of this photograph, there were 178 members, including many of the town's forefathers. (Barton Collection.)

Located on the south side of Broad Street, the Seymour House (built around 1824) was on the stagecoach route between New Haven and Albany. It was a place of much activity, as this was a place for weary travelers to change teams of horses and rest. It was also the chief tavern and hotel for the area. The name changed around 1934 to the Dutch Door Inn and it was decorated to match. It was known as "one of the most popular hostelries in this section of the state," according to the *Tercentenary Pictorial and History of the Lower Naugatuck Valley*. (Barton Collection.)

This advertisement was taken from the *Ansonia, Birmingham, Derby Shelton, and Seymour Directory 1892–1893*. The directory included a general listing of citizens, businesses, streets, town officers, churches, schools, societies, etc. It was published by The Price and Lee Company of New Haven, Connecticut.

76

The Windsor Hotel was one of several available for travelers and businessmen in the area. The hotel was refurbished with modern amenities, such as bathrooms, at the start of the 20th century. It was located at 11 Second Street, across from the old town hall. (Barton Collection.)

The Brunswick Hotel was located at 2 First Street and had 22 rooms, as well as a dining room and café annex. The hotel was well located near the train depot and the business section of town. The building was refurbished in 1902 by the new proprietor, Frank B. McLean.

CONCERT AND BALL,

TO BE GIVEN BY

Nonnawauk Tribe No. 9, I. O. R. M.

AT THE TINGUE OPERA HOUSE,

Friday Evening, April 27, 1906,

MUSIC BY CITIZEN'S ORCHESTRA,

PROF. E. S. COOPER, PROMPTER.

TICKET admitting Gentleman with Lady, **$1.**

EXTRA LADIES' TICKET 50 CENTS EACH

Nonnawauk Tribe No. 9, Improved Order of Red Men, was instituted on May 23, 1887, being named after the old Indian Chieftain Nonnawaug, who is said to have had his headquarters around Watertown, Connecticut. It was originally organized by George Smith, one of the early pharmacists for the town. The tribe had its location at the old Masonic home on Main Street. It was the third oldest tribe in the state, and its mission was to promote benevolence and charity among its members.

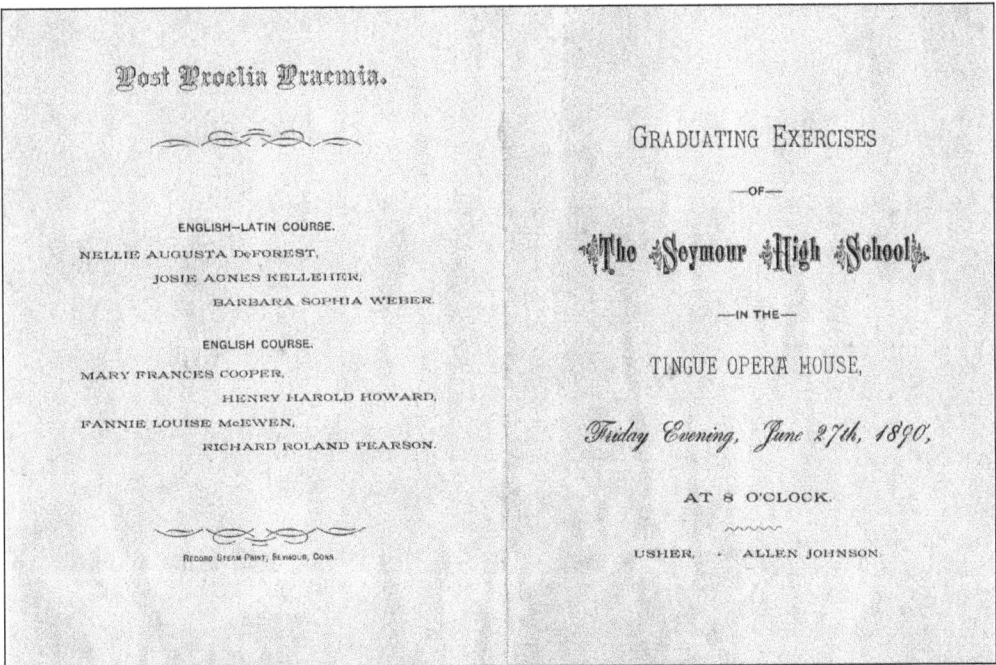

Post Proelia Praemia.

ENGLISH—LATIN COURSE.

NELLIE AUGUSTA DeFOREST,

JOSIE AGNES KELLEHER,

BARBARA SOPHIA WEBER.

ENGLISH COURSE.

MARY FRANCES COOPER,

HENRY HAROLD HOWARD,

FANNIE LOUISE McEWEN,

RICHARD ROLAND PEARSON.

RECORD STEAM PRINT, SEYMOUR, CONN.

GRADUATING EXERCISES

—OF—

The Seymour High School

—IN THE—

TINGUE OPERA HOUSE,

Friday Evening, June 27th, 1890,

AT 8 O'CLOCK.

USHER, · ALLEN JOHNSON.

A program for the Seymour High School class of 1890 outlines graduation exercises. The Tingue Opera House, located downtown, was the site for bringing the townspeople together for recreation and entertainment.

The Tingue Opera House was destroyed by fire on the night of February 4, 1886. The night was a horrendous experience for the Citizens Engine Company firefighters, as the temperature was 8 degrees below zero, and there was a blizzard. Many of the men became coated with ice. The next morning, the hose was found near the building with ice that had formed at a depth of several feet. (Richard Joy.)

These proud firefighters, from left to right, are Fowler Adams, S. Wright, and Harry C. Carpenter. The caption dates the photograph to the late 1800s. They stand posed in their uniforms and full regalia, complete with bugles. The Veterans Firemen's Association, consisting of those who had been active members for 10 years, was formed on July 1, 1900, when Adams and Wright were inducted with 28 other members. (Citizens Engine Company No. 2.)

This early rear view of the Citizens Engine Company was taken after the tower was struck by lightning, which resulted in a large crack. The fire hoses were hung in the tower to dry after being used. There was only one bay that was used for the cart.

This new engine house was built after the annual town meeting on October 4, 1891, appropriated funds to purchase the lot at the corner of Factory and Raymond Streets. The engine house was built with brick and was two stories high with a roomy basement. It was heated by steam and had electricity. (Barton Collection.)

The new firehouse also boasted parlors on the second floor that were handsomely finished. In March 1893, it was decided to raise money to decorate the parlors. The walls received frescoes by H. A. Hurd, and the remainder went towards furniture. (Barton Collection.)

This is an early 1900 photograph of the Citizens Engine Company firemen posing outside of the firehouse for a portrait. The firemen were aided in their work by the large factories, which had powerful rotary force pumps and ample supply of hoses for use in case of a fire. (Barton Collection.)

Originally built as the high school for the town in 1921, this building later became the Seymour Junior High School when a new high school was built on Botsford Road. The building is now known as the Seymour Community Center where the Senior Center and Recreation Department are located. (Seymour Public Library.)

This imposing structure on the corner of Main and DeForest Streets was built in 1918. The neoclassical civic-revival style that it was built in was much like other federal buildings of the time. Today's building code restrictions would inhibit much of the design, as there are many steps and no handicapped-accessible entrance. (Marian K. O'Keefe.)

The oldest school still standing in Seymour dates to 1884 and is located at 100 Bank Street. Throughout the years, many changes have occurred within and to the building. Originally established as both a grade and high school, the building was enlarged with the Annex in 1905 to accommodate an additional eight classrooms. When a new high school was built on Pine Street, Center-Annex remained as a grade school. The original school is now privately owned, while the town retains ownership of the Annex building. (Barton Collection.)

The old Bungay School, located at the corner of Bungay and Canfield Roads, served the youth of the Great Hill section of town. This class photograph was taken in 1928. By the late 1930s, all the old district schools were closed. (R. Stone.)

The final location of the school is on Bungay Road, where it continues to educate children from the Great Hill section of Seymour. The school has had renovations done since this photograph was taken in 1966. (John Felenchak.)

The first Cedar Ridge School was built in 1837. In 1910, the second floor was added, allowing for two classrooms. It was located on Pearl Street, south of Bladen's Brook. The original cost of the building was $175. The site was later home to Seymour Post 5078, Veterans of Foreign Wars, and is currently Veterans Park, which is owned by the Seymour Land and Conservation Trust. (Richard Kisson.)

This Cedar Ridge School third-grade class photograph was taken in mid-1936. From left to right are (first row) Dorothy Abbott, Elizabeth Tong, Rhoda Koehler, Marion Young, and Jeanne Volkmar; (second row) Jack Paige, unknown, Anna Fishem, Ruth Forest, Jane Donovan, Eunise Sargent, Armond Bouchet, and Harold Miller; (third row) Walter Olsen, Francis Gauvin, Keith Mitchell, Kenneth Mitchell, Eurnest Weymer, Jack Volkmar, and Billy Libby; (fourth row) unidentified, Frank Hale, Billy Doll, Bobby Bower, and Robert Thompson.

Maple Street School, located on the corner of Maple and Pearl Streets, was originally built in 1913. Two additions have been added to the building, the most recent in the 1970s to accommodate the growing school population of the district. The school later changed its name to the Anna LoPresti School. (Marian K. O'Keefe.)

One can only wonder why these children were so unhappy. Posing with their teacher on the steps of Maple Street School, the students apparently haven't learned the phrase "say cheese." Button shoes and sailor collars appear to have been the fashion of the day. (Walter Marsh.)

Captured in this teachers photograph taken about 1927 at Maple Street School are (first row) Alice Condon, Cara Greywacz, and Emma McKinnon; (second row) Helen Hamel, Alice Fraher, Agnes Barrett, Ella Burke, Helen Holbrook, and Iris Munson; (third row) Bessie Treat, Edith Beecher, Belle Lockwood, Mary McNerney, Elizabeth Bossidy, Bessie Gorham, Anna LoPresti, and Nellie Ippolito.

In 1949, another group of teachers poses at Maple Street School. From left to right are (first row) Mildred Boyd, Helen Glover, Amy Hillbish, Mary McNerney, Winifred Barton, Barbara Brennan, Helen Hamel, and Alice Condon; (second row) Ruth Larkin, Alice Hurd, Helen Hill, Anna Lane, Suzanne Kelley, Elizabeth Nolan, Bessie Gorham, and Elizabeth Tocher.

The Maple Street Drum Corps is shown in this photograph from around the 1930s–1940s. Four of the students have been identified as Earl Bosworth, Harriet Chatfield, William Gibney, and David O'Connor.

The son of the local family doctor, Thomas Casagrande, is shown standing on the right as his father, "Doc" Casagrande, signs his contract to play for the Philadelphia Phillies as a pitcher in 1947. Casagrande Field was named for Dr. Casagrande. In recent years, the ballfield name was changed to Casagrande-Lang Field to also honor a longtime youth baseball volunteer, Robert Lang. (Felenchuk.)

In 1943, Anna LaCotta stands outside the Strand Theater. The theater was built in 1921 and had an art deco storefront. The marquee is one of the last standing in the state. The theater continues to operate through the Seymour Culture and Arts Commission, showing movies on a weekly basis. (G. Swinik.)

Seymour celebrated its centennial in 1950. Harry Mannweiler was chairman of the executive committee for the organization of activities to mark the event during the latter part of June. There was a pageant, a block dance, a picnic in the park, and a parade. In this photograph, an unidentified resident played the part of an Indian in portraying the town seal. (John Felenchak.)

In a time when dances and balls were the fashion, the Citizens Engine Company celebrated in 1954. This ballroom was decorated and transformed from being just a gymnasium in the old Seymour Middle School. (Citizens Engine Company No. 2.)

92

The Seymour Free Public Library was established in 1892, and it occupied the second floor of the old Town Hall on Second Street. W. C. Sharpe, who authored *Seymour Past and Present* in 1902, was one of the original directors. The library was later located on Pine Street by the Seymour Community Center. During the flood of 1955, the library was destroyed and moved to its current location on Church Street. This photograph captures First Selectman Kenneth Catlin laying the cornerstone of the library in 1958 while Katharine Matthies looks on. (Seymour Public Library.)

The idea of a legion pool was visualized by a legionnaire. The post threw money and muscle into the project, which made a swimming area available in 1926 to hundreds of Seymour youngsters. In addition, Legion Commander George Hummel organized the Seymour Playground Association, which supervised activities for the youth. In 1953, the legion pool became contaminated from local septic systems and was closed to swimming. The dam deteriorated and eventually collapsed. The pond became nothing but a small brook with overgrown brush, a dumping ground, and an eyesore.

In 1989, the Seymour Land Conservation Trust purchased the legion pool with a grant from the Katherine Matthies Foundation. Seymour Trust was the trustee of the foundation at the time, while Cliff Hoyle, William Powanda, and Eugene Coppola were the foundation's first advisory board members. These individuals had the vision and foresight to provide the funds to enable the land trust to preserve this historic and valuable piece of real estate. Although the pool is not open to swimming, members are allowed to fish in the richly stocked waters. (Seymour Land Conservation Trust.)

Five

FLOODING THROUGH
THE YEARS

One of the first recorded floods was in 1891. This photograph was taken from the east side of the Naugatuck River looking over the falls. High up on the hill, the Trinity Church steeple can be seen. (Citizens Fire Department No. 2.)

H. A. Matthews Co. & Little River

Flooding of the Little River near the H. A. Matthews Company in the early 1900s is shown here. Little flood control measures were in place along the many rivers and streams that fed into the Naugatuck River. The H. A. Matthews Company was organized in 1890 and began producing stove trimmings and other hardware at this location. It later expanded to manufacture bicycle parts in 1895. (Citizens Engine Company No. 2.)

The flood that defined Seymour's future occurred during the summer of 1955. Although most people are aware of the flood, many do not know that in addition to the one in August, a second flood, although not as intense, occurred in October. This view is looking from the east side of the Naugatuck River towards the Seymour Lumber Company, pictured in back.

With the bank of the river flooding to the north of Main Street, the flood waters can be seen coming down the street. To the left, Mel's Luncheonette, a pharmacy, and the Seymour Trust Company can be seen.

As workers string a lifeline across Main Street, Chief Francis "Flip" Flaherty stands guard. Chief Flaherty was a beloved figure in the town, both for his standards and fairness in applying the law. A meeting room in town hall, which was at one time the location of the police department, has been named in his honor.

Police and emergency workers carry an elderly woman across Main Street to safety as the flood waters move in. The First National Store, which was located at 127 Main Street and was the first chain supermarket in the town, is pictured in the background. Many people collected the S&H Green Stamps that were given out with purchases, placed them in booklets, and redeemed them for gift items at designated stores. George Bashura, second from left, was a local businessman who repaired shoes.

Looking east across the river toward downtown and the Waterman-Bic building, the falls are nothing but a ripple in the flow of water. The water continued to rise above River Road, which is shown here.

The floodwaters of the Naugatuck River spilled over the banks at the intersection of Main Street and Route 67. At center is a small white building, which was home to the Valley Taxi Company operated by Nicholas Wasko at 150 Main Street. The company continued to operate out of this building until the late 1960s.

The view from Humphreys Street looking north shows the destruction that the flood left at the beginning of Main Street. The river was flush with the train tracks. The Seymour Manufacturing Company can be seen across the river, with the water high above floor level.

Derby Ave   Flood 55

One of the hardest hit residential areas, the homes along Derby Avenue were either destroyed or had substantial damage after the flood of 1955. This view was taken from the railroad tracks on the opposite bank of the river. The home across the river is being torn apart by the force of the water.

from RR on S Main looking toward Derby Ave

As the notation reads, this photograph was taken from South Main Street looking towards Derby Avenue. The immense force of the flood can be seen in the damage that is done to the building at center. The right-hand side of the building is being torn away by the force of the water.

The Little River overflows its banks, flooding the factory to the left before heading into the Naugatuck River. At this level of the flood, the Naugatuck River and Little River meet at the appropriately-named River Street.

The novelty shop manufactured many different products. Some of the items that were produced included household items, such as cake pans. During World War II, the shop made clips for .45-caliber guns. The company was later purchased by the Housatonic Wire Company. This later picture, taken during the flood, shows how high the water rose.

Before and after pictures at the intersection of Derby Avenue and River Street taken from West Street show the damage that was done. The pavement was undermined and destroyed by the force of the waters. Pictured to the left are the Congregational church and Swan Memorial.

Looking east to west down river, the railroad bridge that spanned the river has been destroyed and swept away during the flood. The trestle over Route 67 stands alone as the roadway is completely obliterated. Directly below the trestle, the lower outline of the Bank Street bridge can be seen. It would take several months before train service could be restarted in the region.

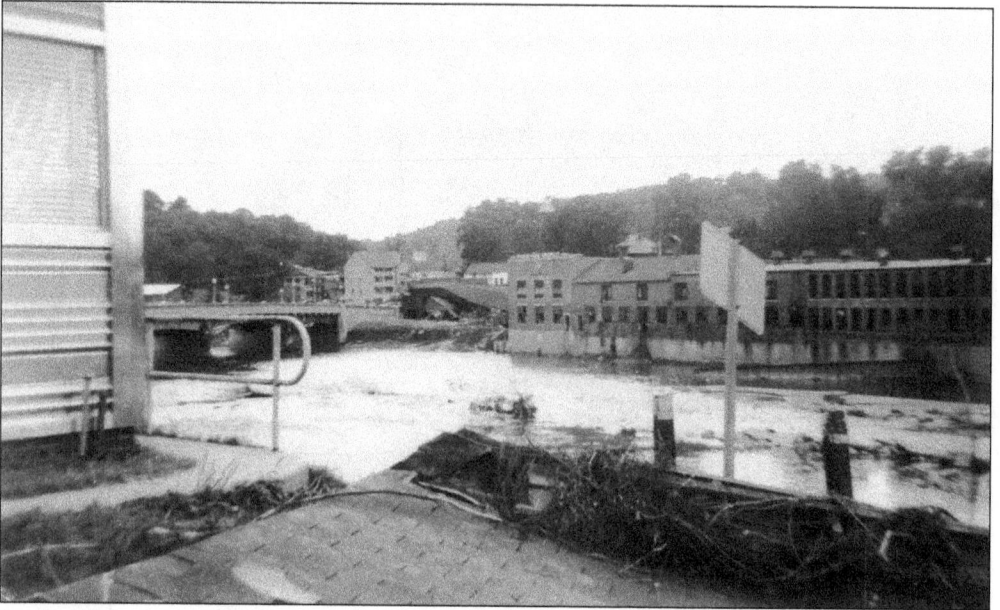

Looking west across the Bank Street bridge, a building to the left of the bridge is destroyed from the flood. On the left is Joe's Diner, which was operated by Joseph A. Syombathy and which would later become Tony's Diner. At the bottom of the photograph, a piece of a building comes to rest in the parking lot.

The Ward Funeral Home and Seymour High School are seen across Broad Street. The homes that were in the location of Pine Street were never rebuilt. The funeral home also moved its location. Only two buildings remain standing from this period: the community center and the Congregational church.

With the receding of the waters, the damage was quickly assessed. Kerite's location at the corner of Day Street and Main Street was across from the river. Utility lines and poles were damaged, along with the roadways. Visible at the bottom of the photograph are all the footprints that were left behind in the mud. In the background is downtown Seymour's Main Street.

The steel Broad Street bridge spanning the Naugatuck River was destroyed by the water, trees, and other debris that came down the river. The new concrete bridge that replaced it was engineered longer and higher. Unfortunately, due to the arch of the bridge, the rocks and falls can no longer be easily viewed. (John Felenchak.)

The original Seymour Free Public Library, which was located at the corner of Pine and Broad Streets, was destroyed in the flood of 1955. This photograph was taken after the flood, showing the destroyed library.

The time is recorded on the clock of the Seymour Manufacturing Company on the west side of the river during the flood of 1955. The company manufactured nickel silver and phosphor bronze in sheets, wire, and rod, as well as nickel anodes, supplying a large percentage of our country's total production of these items.

Although flood controls were put in place after the floods of 1955, Seymour continued to experience flooding from small streams and rivers. This photograph, taken during the 1982 flood, shows a part of Derby Avenue with people waist deep in water. Route 8 is in the background.

Beach Street continued to be an area of flooding as the Paper Mill Pond overflows its banks with the waters of Bladen's Brook as recently as 1982. At the top right is the old paper mill.

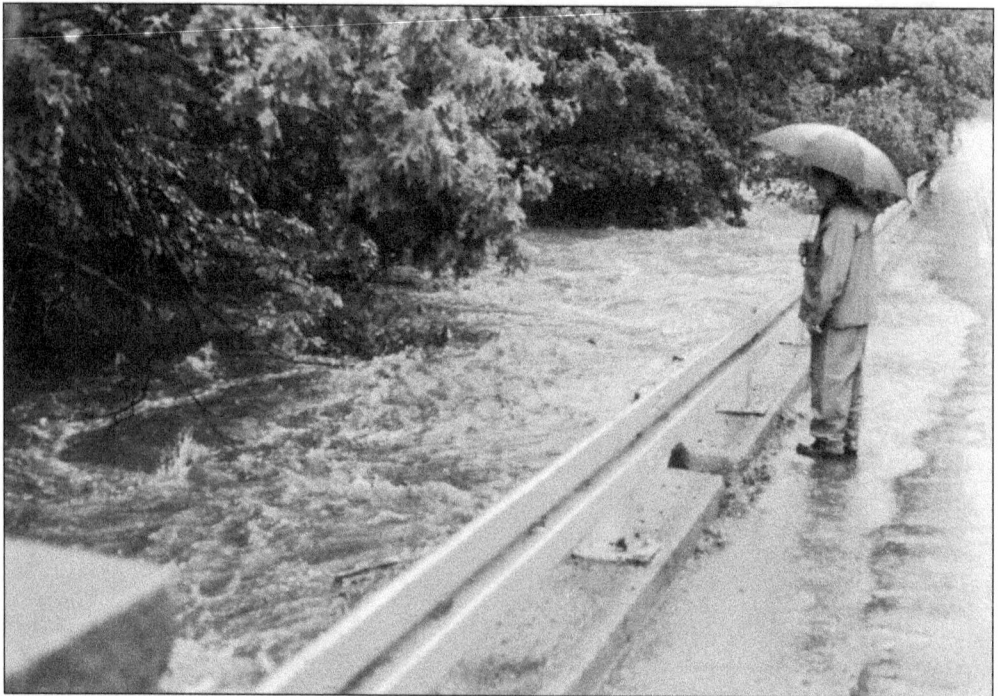

An onlooker watches the rising Bladen's Brook along Route 67 during the height of the flood. Floods such as this were often known as freshets, which means a sudden rise of a river or stream due to heavy rains or rapid melting of ice or snow.

Six

A COMMUNITY AFTER THE FLOOD

Celebrating Memorial Day with a parade, students from Center School are seen marching to French Memorial Park in 1959. Patriotism was encouraged, as many of these youth had parents who recently returned from the Korean conflict.

The Young Marines of the Valley was one of many youth organizations in the town. Weekly drills were held, and the group also participated in parades. This 1965 photograph shows a large group of youth receiving instruction from their drill sergeant prior to marching in a parade.

The Valley Detachment Marine Corps League has been active in the Valley since the 1960s, when it was able to obtain the Lutheran church on West Street for its home base. The League put on many functions for its members, including family events, such as dances, The Young Marines of the Valley, and the first Christmas party held at the League home in 1968.

This view looking north on Main Street in the late 1960s shows a town in need of revitalization. A plan was developed to improve the town in the early 1990s. Assisting in the process were grants from the Katharine Matthies Foundation, the Community Foundation of New Haven, and the Department of Economic and Community Development. Shown in this picture is the Seymour Trust Company on the lower left, a boarded-up building, Isaacson's family clothing store, and the Tingue building. On the right is the train station. The train station was removed in the 1970s, and a parking lot was put in its place.

Great Hill Hose Company, which was established in 1947 to service the Great Hill section of Seymour, partakes in the annual Memorial Day Parade on Main Street (the train station is to the left). The first meeting elected the following officers: Capt. Walter Bomba, 1st Lt. Clifford Strumello, 2nd Lt. John Sypniewski, Secretary Roy Cauxx, and Treasurer Gilbert Nash. Ralph Ajello later became the engineer of the company. (John Felenchak.)

A local carnival was sponsored by the Citizens Engine Company No. 2 during the 1960s. The carnival's location was in the Wakely Street parking lot, adjacent to the Naugatuck River and Tingue Falls. Held as a fundraiser, the carnival provided much-needed funds for the volunteer organization while providing an affordable outing for many families. (Citizens Engine Company No. 2.)

Taken in 1973, this photograph shows DeForest Street, formerly known as Factory Street, prior to the expansion of the firehouse. There had been two homes between the firehouse and the town hall. In March 1975, construction was begun to enlarge the firehouse to include four new bays to house the apparatus. (Citizens Engine Company No. 2.)

114

Affectionately known as Miss LoPresti, Anna LoPresti made a lasting imprint on the town. She was a woman who spent her life working with and helping other people. Most of her years were spent at the Maple Street School, first as a teacher and then as a principal. She was also the principal of Center School and Chatfield School. After retirement, she became the first woman selectman for the town from 1973 to 1977. Her legacy was having her beloved school's name changed to the Anna L. LoPresti School.

HER NAME IS ANNA

SOME KNOW HER AS ANN
SOME KNOW HER AS MISS LoPRESTI
SHE HOPES THAT AFTER NOVEMBER 6
EVERYONE WILL KNOW HER AS
FIRST SELECTMAN OF SEYMOUR

Seymour took part in many of the festivities of our nation's bicentennial celebration in 1976. The town formed a bicentennial committee whose duties included striking a town bicentennial coin honoring the occasion. The festivities culminated with a bicentennial ball in New Haven, where Paul Haluschak, bicentennial chairman, dances with Ann Conroy. They dressed in period clothing to celebrate the event.

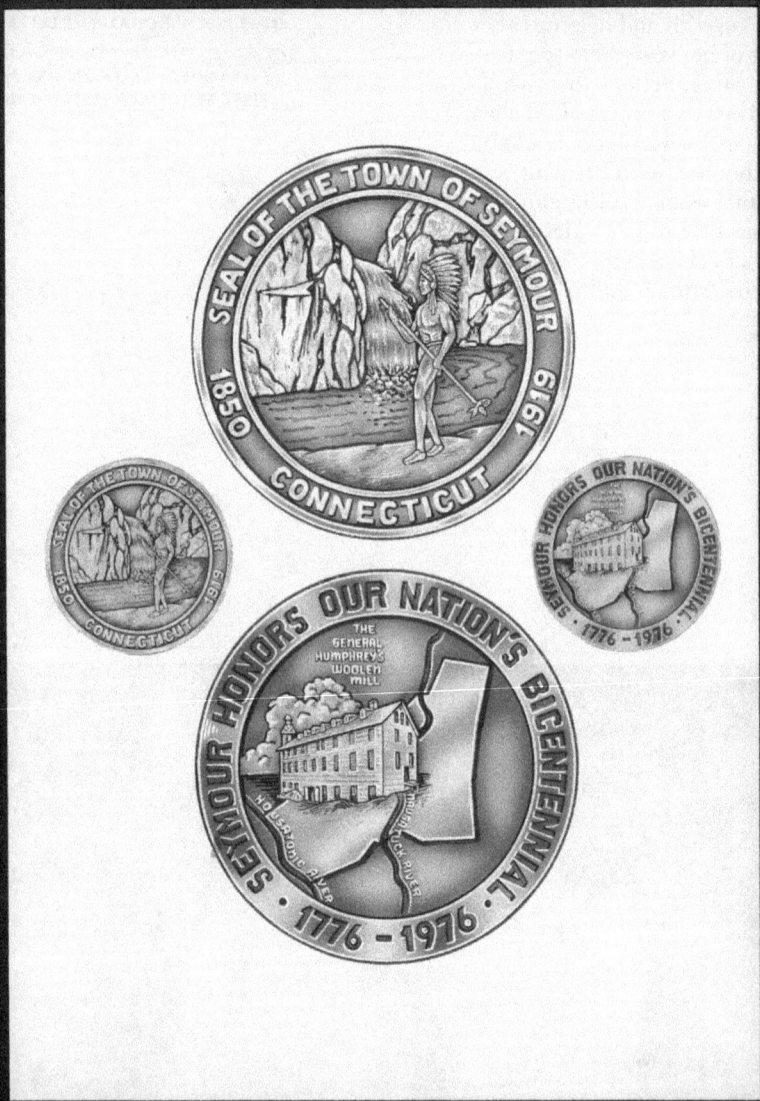

The board of selectmen voted in 1919 to use this image of an Indian standing beside the Tingue Falls on the Naugatuck River as the town seal. During the 1980s, the town adopted a different symbol, the historic bell tower at the Citizens Engine Company, and placed it on letterheads and signs. In 2000, it was learned that there had never been a seal registered with the secretary of state's office. During that year, the town celebrated its 150th anniversary and officially registered the original seal with the state. It depicts what is believed to be Joseph Mawehu Chuse, leader of the Indian village, near the waterfall during early European settlement.

The original Klarides Supermarket was located at 271 Bank Street and was listed in the 1920 Seymour directory as a supplier of flour and groceries. Before most stores were open on Sundays in the 1960s, the Klarides family remained open until early afternoon, making it a busy venue after church. The store was known for its hometown friendliness. (James Zepos.)

In 1972, the Klarides family developed the site directly behind their original store and called it Klarides Village. The new IGA Klarides provided residents with more selection, including an appliance section. With the expansion came a restaurant, a Laundromat, and other small retail businesses. They further expanded the site eastward on their property with more stores. In 1996, Klarides Supermarket was sold to Stop and Shop. (James Zepos.)

A northern view from the Trestle Tavern parking lot in the early 1970s looks up Main Street from the intersection of Broad Street. At the top of the picture is the Seymour post office. The tall building to the left is the Waterman-Bic building. The billboards on top of the building continue to advertise to drivers on Route 8.

The Seymour Pumpkin Festival is an annual event held in September at French Memorial Park. It was started in 1965 by an all-volunteer committee functioning as a nonprofit organization. Featured activities include rides, contests, and prizes for youngsters, as well as arts and crafts and food booths. The festival gives local organizations the opportunity to raise funds. All net profits are given to worthwhile organizations in the community.

This sign erected at Broad Street Park in 1978 by the Town of Seymour, the Seymour Historical Society, and the Connecticut Historical Commission gives visitors a brief history of the town from its beginnings in 1650 to 1850. (Marian K. O'Keefe.)

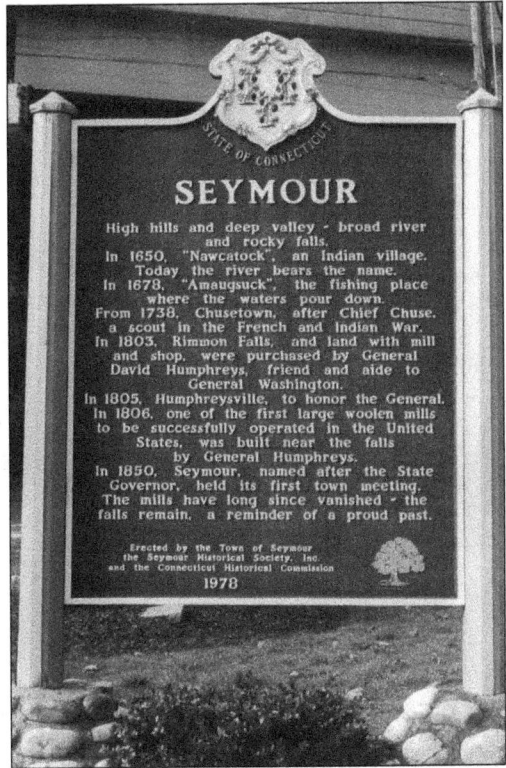

STATE OF CONNECTICUT

SEYMOUR

High hills and deep valley - broad river and rocky falls.
In 1650, "Nawcatock", an Indian village. Today the river bears the name.
In 1678, "Amaugsuck", the fishing place where the waters pour down.
From 1738, Chusetown, after Chief Chuse, a scout in the French and Indian War.
In 1803, Rimmon Falls, and land with mill and shop, were purchased by General David Humphreys, friend and aide to General Washington.
In 1805, Humphreysville, to honor the General.
In 1806, one of the first large woolen mills to be successfully operated in the United States, was built near the falls by General Humphreys.
In 1850, Seymour, named after the State Governor, held its first town meeting. The mills have long since vanished - the falls remain, a reminder of a proud past.

Erected by the Town of Seymour the Seymour Historical Society, Inc. and the Connecticut Historical Commission
1978

The Seymour High School marching band steps out in full regalia, proudly wearing the school colors of blue and gold. This group of highly skilled musicians was featured in the 1979 Memorial Day Parade. In addition to the band, there was a full complement of majorettes and a pompom squad. The band also participated in other local parades. (John Felenchak.)

An opportunity for economic development came during the early 1980s with the groundbreaking of the Silvermine Industrial Park on Silvermine Road on the east side of town. The site contained 125 acres available for manufacturing businesses of all types. At the groundbreaking was Gov. William O'Neill, second from left, along with other local dignitaries.

The Seymour Specialty Wire Company organized an employee buyout to create the largest democratically owned industrial firm in the nation from 1984 to 1991. Prior to the company closing, the movie *Other People's Money* used the site for filming. It was originally known as the Seymour Manufacturing Company. (John Felenchak.)

The new Seymour Town Hall expansion was completed during the 1980s to allow for more office space and a large meeting room named in honor of Norma Drummer, who was the longtime town clerk. On the right is the back entry to Isaacson's, a well-known family clothing store. In the shopping plaza to the left, Pieroway's, a furniture store, was located at the site of former food stores including Finest and Foodland. Route 8 traverses the top of the picture, with Seymour Specialty Wire in the far background.

Long before gas and diesel fire engines, this horse-drawn 1884 Button Steamer was the first fire apparatus the Citizens Fire Company used to fight fires. The Button Steamer's inventor was Lysander Button, who was born in North Haven, Connecticut. This photograph was taken coming up Main Street by the post office. (John Felenchak.)

The summer of 1984 found Elaine Brandon in front of the old Firestone store on Main Street. The caption notes that they had just removed the façade, revealing the old title, and that she had stood for this picture for posterity. The building was originally built in 1900 and is an important part of the Seymour streetscape.

This aerial view of downtown Seymour highlights many natural and man-made resources available to the town. At the upper left, the community center sits at the site of the former high/middle school location, with the Congregational church's white steeple highlighted. Traversing the river is the Broad Street bridge, while Route 8 flows from the bottom right to the top left corner. In the upper middle, the white waters cascading over the Tingue Falls dam are seen flowing downstream in the Naugatuck River. Center left is the New Haven copper factory, which is adjacent to the old Waterman Pen Company Complex (now apartments). Center right is Seymour Town Hall and the Citizens Engine Company No. 2 complex. The white roof of the angular post office is shown on the bottom middle.

This model of the old covered bridge that crossed the Naugatuck River at Bank Street was originally located in French Memorial Park. Later it was moved to the Broad Street Park site. (Marian K. O'Keefe.)

Broad Street Park is located on the west side of the Naugatuck River at the intersection of River and West Streets. It has been undergoing continuing restoration for a tribute to Korea and Vietnam veterans. (Marian K. O'Keefe.)

The original Veteran's Memorial Grove was located just inside the entrance to the French Memorial Park. The rock formation bandstand is still in use for summer concerts sponsored by the Seymour Culture and Arts Commission. The Civil War monument is on the left looking out over downtown Seymour.

The dedication of the new Veteran's Memorial Grove at French Memorial Park commenced on June 10, 1990. The grove honors the town's fallen heroes and is the site of annual Memorial Day and Veterans Day ceremonies. The proud members of Emil Senger Post 10, American Legion, are pictured here at the ceremony. Post 10 was established in 1923 and named Emil Senger for the first World War I casualty from Seymour.

The making of *Other People's Money* brought movie stars to Seymour in 1990. The premise of the film, starring Danny DeVito and Gregory Peck, was a hostile takeover of a mom-and-pop company. Seymour Specialty Wire was the main location, along with other downtown venues. Dean Jones played Bill Coles and was the grand marshall of the Seymour Christmas Parade, the only parade of its type in the state. (Robert Lang.)

The Seymour Culture and Arts Commission is responsible for many community events. During the past decade, they have been sponsoring downtown block party dances, where good times are had by both young and old. In this photograph, residents can be seen dancing on Main Street (Bank Street is on the right.)

Seymour's downtown area has been attracting many antique dealers and unique stores with its recent revitalization. First Saturdays offer shoppers special events. Community spirit is shown by volunteers helping to keep the area attractive. Store owner Sam Mirlis is shown heading up a team of volunteers.

Citizens Engine Company No. 2 celebrated its 125th anniversary with a juried parade in the summer of 2009. The parade featured fire companies throughout the state. On the reviewing stand are Selectman Francis Conroy, First Selectman Robert Koskelowski, Fire Parade Marshall Jonathan Ertman, State Representative Theresa Conroy, and Selectman Paul Roy.

Visit us at
arcadiapublishing.com

www.ingramcontent.com/pod-product-compliance
Lightning Source LLC
Chambersburg PA
CBHW050552110426
42813CB00008B/2337